Ta'Mara's
Divine Creation

Ta'Mara T. Beaulieu

ISBN 978-93-5610-390-0
© Ta'Mara T. Beaulieu 2022
Published in India 2022 by Pencil

Contributors:
Editor: Michael "Mike Gutta" Gibson
Editor: Diane "Teenie" Bell
Editor: Michael "Mike Gutta" Gibson
Editor: Diane "Teenie" Bell

A brand of
One Point Six Technologies Pvt. Ltd.
123, Building J2, Shram Seva Premises,
Wadala Truck Terminal, Wadala (E)
Mumbai 400037, Maharashtra, INDIA
E connect@thepencilapp.com
W www.thepencilapp.com

Author biography

Ta'Mara T. Beaulieu born & raised in Baton Rouge, LA. She began writing in 2018, about how to reach her Divine Higher Self due to past trauma, abuse, and family death and addictions that she had to deal with throught out her child hood and adult hood, life was one the edge for her, to save herself Ta'Mara used every term in her book to practice everything to become who she is today by transitioning her self to strive beyond her insurcurities, mind, body and soul with all GOD'S power. She is a mother of five beautiful children four boys and one girl. This is Ta'Mara's first book!

CONTENTS

Divine Creation

Begins....

Biorhythm

A cycle in the physiology or functioning an orgasism, such as the daily cycle of sleeping and walking.

A cycle pattern of physical, emotional, or mental activity said to occur in the life of a person.

Biorhythm are based on the idea that a persons life is on a cycle with peaks and troughs. It breaks down the physical, spiritual, the emotional and intellectual.

Physical cycle follows 23 day period, and focuses on stamina, health, and strength. The emotional cycle follows 28 day period and is related to creativity, emotions, and intuition.

Finally, the intellectual cycle lasts 33 days and is associated with THINKING, JUDGEMENT, & CONCENTRATION.

222

Angel Number

Angel Number

The devine forces are sending you an encoragement to pursue dreams and goals you have set up for yourself.

A sign of personal growth, expansion and new opportunities of personal growth and helps you achieve a state of harmony and balance in your life, manifesting miracles and opportunities that signifies that you are blessed with an abundance of gifts and future opportunities are yours for the taking, spiritual enlightenment and trusting the sacred energies.

LOVE / RELATIONS

#2 Has qualities for a perfect relationship or partnership bring two people together and balancing their needs and expectations. It ensures harmony , something thst is vital for a successful relationship.

333

Right Path

You're on the right path, the angels are around us to remove all negativity in your minds, and fill with perfect love.

The guardian angels are always here to help you when you're in need. Our prayers have been heard and answered.

333 represents Mind, Body & Spirit, and is the threefold nature of divinity.

444

Stay Focused

Your Prayers have been heard and answered and the universe encourages you to stay focused to finish the job.

444 represents that you may already have a strong connection with the angels and source and you are on a path of spiritual awakening.

Signifies thats you are in love and that your inner wisdom has been pointing you in the right direction. You have nothing to fear in regards to your life, work and divine life purpose.

555

Positive & Confident

Reveals you should stay positive and confident about the changes around you because the angels are headed your way with a vibrant spiritual wind covering your life.

666

Negativity

"DANGER" is near!
"Negativity" is around!

777

Energetic Alignment

You are in energetic alignment with the universe and are in perfect vibrational match to bringing in blessings, miracles, good luck, happiness, abundance, great opportunities, and a sign of your dreams coming true. You have listened to divine guidance and are now putting that wisdom to work in your life.

Begin to open up your heart. The angels are supporting you in whatever you decide to do.

- You and your twin-flame are going through a period of transformation.

New Beginnings, Abundance, Positive Energy, you are destined for something GREAT. Now it's time to find out and manifest your life goals a big support from "GOD".

1222

Powerful Signs

A powerful sign that you are to step out of your comfort zone and take a new direction to begin new projects, universal energies and the angels are working behind the scenes of following your career path bares a message of faithfulness.

- Angels are noticing your effort and progress.

- Urges you to have a high expectation and think of the highest possible goals for you because the universal are your guides.

1244

Boosts of Self

- You need to see yourself in a higher, better, and brighter light. Your angels are helping you to boosts your self-esteem.

- Acknowledge the determination, discipline, and hardwork you put into your endeavors in the past, achieve your happiness. The secret language of color healing.

- Colors are used for general guidance, ask the questions in order to get answers and use it for healing. Color is extremely spiritual and very important in healing. It comes with a bold rainbow on the front. This matches the energy on the deck and you really feel the power of colors when holding the box in your hands.

1144

Move Forward

Is especially potent as it relates to love and romantic relationships, Therefore 11:44 asks you to stay open in your existing relationship or new relationship and move forward with "FAITH"

1255

The Chosen One

A message from your inner self telling you to volunteer for a cause, project, or community work that has meaning to you. Get rid of old and let positivity serve you. Get ready for wonderful changes.

A clear sign that guardian angels are thinking of you right now. They want to relay to you that you have been "CHOSEN".

Serve those people who need your help. It signifies affection towards everyone you know.

Angels of Power

Arch-Angels

<u>Archangel Ariel</u>- Lioness of god. Her energy is powerful, oversees environmental causes, and yet gentle. She is known to be a guardian and healer of animals. She provides such needs as shelter, money, and supplies.

<u>Archangel Azrael</u>- Whom God helps, His entergy is calm and patient, helps people heal from grief.

<u>Archangel Gabriel</u>- Messenger of God, she is aligned with child vearing and pregnancy she is faminine.

The <u>Archangel Metatron</u>has the special ability to connect with the humans who seek his guidance and protection.

- Angel of empowerment

- He is believed to have risen into the angelic kingdom from a human incarnation on earth, along with his spiritual brother.

The **<u>Archangel Sandalphan,</u>** Archangel Metatron is revered as one of the most powerful archangels because he represents the ability that we have to access our spiritual power and achieve ascension into heaven.

Archangel Metatron sits beside god in heaven, providing

guidance to the cherubs and seraphim, he's also known as the Angel of Divine presence and the Chancellor of Heaven.

Archangel Sandalphan

- Learning any musical instrument an singing, poetry

- Performance arts, acting, dancing and singing, prayer, self confidence, finding and developing

- Social work, especially involving children and families, spiritual development

- Assists with higher communication

- Prayers made to him are answered in music

Archangel Michael

is the chief prince of the heavenlyness, Michael plays a significant part in the end-time events. He leads a host of angels in a victorious war over satan and his demons in revelation 12. He's not merly an angel but he's the head of a battalion of angels. His name means who is like "GOD".

The human incarnation of white, green, deep pink spiritual colors. Metatron is believed to have been enoch, the biblical scribe and prophet known as one of the only two angels who was first a human when he ascended into the angelic realm, Metatron was given one of the most task in heaven to record the choices made on earth and in heaven into a universal archive known as the Akashic record or the Book of Life.

By working with archangel metatron (leader of all angels) to access your records in the book of life, I will learn where i came from, where i am now, and where i am going. (Gabriel, Michael, Raphael = all arch-angels)

- Smells- pepper, chilles, sweetly floral, or a strong herbal smell

- Colors- white, green, deep pink, rainbow

Archangel Michael

- Glory of God provides guidance to those who seek to develop and gain their intuition.

Archangel Jeremiel

- Mercy of God. Helps you see light in every situation can plan for positive change.

Archangel Jophiel

- Beauty of God helps heal negativity helps us see beauty in our enviornment.

Archangel Metatron

- Highest of Angels

Archangel Michael

- He who is like GOD

Archangel Chamuel

- He who sees GOD enables you to see vision. The connection between everyone and everything.

Archangel Raquel

- Friend of GOD. He assist with legal matters.

Archangel Raphael

- He who heals. He guides those who heal others.

Archangel Raziel

- Secrets of GOD. He Imbodies divine wisdom.

Archangel Uriel

- Light of GOD. Righteousness of GOD, reminds us to be GREATFUL.

Archangel Metatron

is strongly linked to the number 11, 11:11 is a clear sign that you are being supported by metatron. He can only help if we ask.

After i ask archangel metatron for his help with any area in my life, I must simply trust that the way forward will be shown to me. Intuitive nudges, synchronicities, and sudden impulses can be a sign that i am being guided.

When i meditate, archangel metatron appears as a mighty celestial being who is surrounded by a bright light.

He has multiple sets of golden wings and he is dressed in a bright blue robe with the faded magenta layering on top, also dressed in dark green and bright pink.
He can also intercede on our behalf on our behlaf using unlimited power of the metatron cube.

In order to connect with him contact him and listen to what he has to say. I will need to quiet your mind and raise your entergy. The quickest way to do this is through meditation.

When i contact metatron, it is extrememly easy, either mentally or orally. All i need to do is let him know why you need his help.

Permit my soul to express itself and reach communication with archangel metatron because metatron is so intune qith hummanity and already knows everything about our lives, there is a good chance that he already knows the kinds of help that i require.

If you concentrate on the symbol and imagine that it is spinning clockwise, it will allow you to pull positive entergy from the universe into myself and dispense negative entergy at the same time.

1212

Growth and Development

- Growth and development and suggest that the angels want you to make positive changes in my life. Everyday is a new chance to succeed be brave and find my life purpose goal.

- Believing in myself and my abilities is the first step towards inner peace and happiness, when i do this the rest will fall into place.

- Give myself quality time alone, spending time on myself, and my hobbies are important.

- Believing in myself and my abilities is the first step towards inner peace and happiness, growth, change and rebirth.

- Spend time working on my roots and relationship, Allow myself to trust the people around me and spend quality time with my family.

Communicating with Spirit Guides

Concentrate

- Concentrate on my inner voice as well as whatever sign i think may have come from my spirit guide.

- Meditate in absolute silence and involve the ability to focus on nothing rather than constant stream of thoughts happening in our heads.

- If i am able to be still and quiet this could pave the way for an honest and true conversation with our spirit guides. I may be more aware of messages or signs while meditation. It will bring me closer spiritually to the other side.

- If i notice voices or items moving in my home, this is a particularly powerful sign and should be noted. Spirit guides have something extremely urgently to tell me.

Learning How To Listen To My Spirit Guides

Trust & Believe

- Trust what I am hearing and believe that my spirit guides have something to tell me.

- This can feel a little silly at first

- Be kind to myself

- Ask the universe my question, including what my guardians maybe trying to tell me.

- Take a pause and listen, you may recieve an answer right away or I may have to wait for sometime.

- Sometime i will get the answer when i least expected it.

Telepathy Gift

Teleportation

- Passed down from ancient ancestors we all have the innate ability to connect with the conciousness of others.

- Telepathy is the process of receiving thoughts or feelings from another person.

- It usually happens over distance and without the use of other senses like hearing or touch.

6666

Strong Talent

- Indicates an extremely strong talent for the healing arts. It is healing strength that comes through the link I've created between my mind and heart.

- My heart is full of love and compassion.

- Ability to use imagination and intellect together for positive outcomes.

- Focus more on my partner

1026

My Birthday

I am successfully manifesting my financial flow and material supply in order to sustain and maintain me along the way.

1026

- Stands for peace and harmony, the angels are playing an important role in my life.

- My thoughts are connected to the angels

Manifestation

Abstract Ideas

An event, action or object that clearly shows or embodies somethinbg, especially a theory or abstract idea.

Divine Creation

Beliefs of the Universe

Creationism, the belief that the universe and the various forms of life were created by god out of nothing. It is a response primarily to modern evolutionary theory, which explains the diversity of life without recourse to the doctrine of god or any other divine power. God created man and trees and the light on its way from the stars in their observed slate, so too they can know that the world was created over the six days of creation that reflects progression to its currently-observed slate with understanding the physical ways to the universe.

The whole cosmic system of matter and entergy of which earth and therefore the human race is apart. Humanity has traveled a long road since societies imagined earth, the un, and the moon as the main objects of creation with the rest of the universe formed almost as an after-thought.

Fruits of the Spirit

Undisturbed Meaning

<u>Joy</u> - is the state of being undisturbed by the negative things in life by turning all negative thoughts into positivity and focus on the presence with nothing but love.

<u>Peace</u> - is tranquility in our soul that comes from relying on God / innerself. The key is to trust god in the unseen realm. Meditate on your future with love while living in the presence.

<u>Patience</u> - is the ability to bare the imperfections of other people through the knowledge of our own imperfections and our needs for god's mercy and forgivness.

<u>Kindness</u>- the willingess to forgive others above and beyond of what we expect them because negative things, sayings or objects can create mental blocks, confusion, and set backs.

<u>Goodness</u> - the avoidance of evil and the embrace of whats right even at the outcome of an individuals earthly fame and fortune.

<u>Long Suffering</u>- is patience under provocation. It is to endure quietly and from the attacks of others.

<u>Gentleness</u>- is to be forgiving rather than angry, gracious rather than seeking revenge, always be gentle with love and humble at heart.

Modesty- is humbling yourself acknowledging that any of your successe, achievements, talents, are not truly your own but gifts from God.

Faith- is a fruit of the holy spirit which means living in our own accordance with god's will for our life at all times.

Self Control- is continuence its not a saying to deny yourself of what you need or want, long as what you want is good. It is the exercise of moderation in all things.

Love- is the love of God and of your neighbor, without any thought of anything in return. Charity is expressed in concrete action towards God and others.

Faithfulness- comes from a place of trust and loyalty. It requires us to submit our ways to God realizing that we are in need of a savior and that he is in control of our lives.

Sacrifce- is an offering to God or to a divine or a supernatural figure. The destruction of surrender of something for the sake of something else.

Unity- is related to the spiritual soul and not to the physical nature or matter relating characteristic of sacred things, the church, religion, and standing in a relationship based on communication between the souls or minds of the person.

Repent- to turn from sin and dedicate oneself to the amendment of one's life to confess and apologize for your sins or to feed remorseful about things you have done wrong.

Principals of Repentance

Confessions

Acknowledge your sins, confess your shame and your guilt. Then plead with him to help you though triumph. **_Brothers and Sisters_**, we must take our own sins to christ, willing to stand up for what is right in the sight of God, even if it means accepting rejection and death. The gift of courage allows people the firmness of mind that is required both in doing good and in enduring evil especially with regards to goods or evils that are difficult.

Knowledge- is the gift of understanding the meaning of God, the gift of knowledge is more than a accumulation of facts.

Piety- with the gift of reverence something called piety, we have a deep sense of respect for God and the church. A person with reverence recognizes our total reliance on God and comes before God with humility, trust, and love. Piety is the gift whereby at the holy spirits instigation we pay worship and duty to God as our fathrer, the lord in humble and sorrowful repentance. We must plead with for power then overcome them.

6 Steps of Repentance

Commandments of Confession

- We must feel sorrow for our sins

- We must forsake our sins

- We must confess our sins

- We must make restitution

- We must forgive others

- We must keep the commandments of God

Seven Gifts of the Holy Spirit

GOD gives GIFTS

- ___Wisdom___is the gift God gives us to see his work in our lives and in the world. For the wise person, the wonders of nature, historical events, and the ups and downs of our lives take on deeper meaning. The matters of judgement about the truth, and being able to see the whole image of God. We see God as our father and other people with dignity. Lastly being able to see God in everyone and everything, Everywhere!

- ___Understanding___in understanding we comprehend how we need to live as a follower of christ. A person with understanding is not confused by all the conflicting messages in our culture about the right way to live. The gift of unerstanding perfects a speculative reason in the apprehension of trurh. It is the gift whereby self-evident principles are known.

- ___Counsel(right judgement)___With the gift of counsel / right judgement, we know the difference between right and wrong and we choose to do whats right. A person with right judgement avoinds sin and lives out the values taught by jesus.The gift of truth that allows the person to respond prudently and happily to believe of Christ the Lord.

- **Fortitude(*coverage*)**With this gift we overcome our fear and are willing to take risk as a follower of Jesus Christ. A person with coverage.

- ***Fear of the Lord***The gift of fear of the Lord we are aware of the glory and majesty of God. A person with wonder and swe knows that God is the perfection of all we desire, perfection of all we desire, perfect knowledge and perfect goodness, perfect power and perfect love. This gift is described by Aquinas as fear of God. He describes the gift as a (filial fear) like a childs fear or punishment. Fear of the Lord is the beginning of wisdom because it puts our mindset in its correct location with respect to God, we are the finite, dependent creatures, and he is infinite, all powerful creator. Knowing God is all powerful.

- The gift of wisdom corresponds to the virtue of charity.

- The gift of understanding corresponds to the virtue of faith.

- The gift of counsel (right judgement) corresponds to the virtue of fortitude.

- The gift of knowledge corresponds to the virtue of justice.

- The gift of wonder and awe corresponds to the virtue of temperance

  o

Indian Commandments

10 Commandment Terms

I.   Put God first

II.   Use Gods name with respect

III.   Go to church on the Sabbath day and make it a day for family

IV.   Love, respect and obey your parents

V.   Respect human life, dont kill

VI.   Be faithful to your husband or wife

VII.   Do not steal or take things that do not belong to you

VIII.   Always speak the truth and do not lie

IX.   Dont take anyones goods

X.   Do not go after ones wife or husband

10 Commandments KJV

- I am the Lord thy God, thou shall not have any God before me

- Thou shalt not take the name of the Lord thy God in vein

- Keep holy on the Sabbath day

- Honor thy Mother and Father

- Thou shalt not kill

- Thou shalt not steal

- Thou shalt not bear false witness against thy neighbor

- Thou shalt not covet thy neighbors wife

- Thou shalt not covet thy neighbors goods

The Meanings of Angel Numbers

- 000 - Opportunity awaits

- 111 - Put yourself out therew j

- 222 - Find steadier footing

- 333 - Explore what you have to offer

- 444 - Face things head on

- 555 - It is time for transformation

- 666 - Look at things in a new way

- 777 - New opportunities has arose

- 888 - Divine spiritual support from universal angel

- 999 - You'll soon begin a new journey

- ***0000*** Zero is new things taken place, you're at the very beginning of a brand new cycle, which means you can create whatever your heart desires. Dont be afraid to make big old decisions at this point in your journey.

- *1111-* One is a power manifestation figure, relish an opporturnityy to make a wish, set an intention, plant a seed as this believed to indicate a green light from the universe. You are working with exraordinary support from your angels,guides or anestors so, at that moment, the present and future are dynamically connected.

- *2222-* Two, suggest balance, trust and alignment. It means someone in the physical realm or spiritual realm /////////// excellent time to reach out to your most trusted companion to see if divine collaboration is possible.

- *3333-* Three is an indicationof magnetic creativity, you have the creativity to add your unique talents and abilities to a situation and leaning into your innate gifts. You'll find more value and abundance in whatever circumstances you are navigating. Your artistic expressions are critical!

- *4444-* Four is stablelization. You are in the process of grounding, rooting and cultivating an infrastructure thats truly built to last. Dont be afraid to ask for help or assistance, especially if you;re navigating long-term projects that require specific expertise. Fundamentally, this is about establishing trust that will empower you to reach new heights

- *5555-* Five is major changes on the horizon. If you've been feeling stuck, stifled or inspired reveals that massive shifts are in the works. This means transformations are occuring behind the scenes. In other words, key decision makers are still weighing options, but, you're surely on the right path.

- *6666* Six is the number most may fear because of religious associations with the devil or demon figure within the angel numbers. It has an supportive compassionate and empathetice nature. Six is gentle, much needed reminder to treat yourself with kindness and understanting. Some things may not go according to planned but with angel numner 6 on your side you can choose how you want to interpret a situation, remembering that everything happens for a reason.

- *7777*- Seven is the luxurious blessed angel number. Meaning good forturne, especially finance - wine, could be on the way. New monetary opportunities ma arise. So seven invites you to branch out and explore possibilities beyond your comfort zone. Short term gigs may become lucrative, consistent income streams. So, intergrating your spiritual with your values i the perfect expression of theis energy.

- *8888* Eight is the most divine number, it reflects a connection to the spiritual universe in a powerful way. Those who believe in a afterlife may see eights as a sign that they're receivig supernatural support from love ones who've crossed on. Donyt be afraid to dive into your intuition

- ***9999*** Nine is the final digit in the numerology. The presence of 9 suggest a chapter may be comign to an end, means a meaningful cycle could come to a close and you'll soon be beginning a brand new journey. This is an excellent time to step outside your comfort zone, expand your horizons and explore new territory, wheather you're interested in venturing into a new career or going back to school. The spiritual universe will be sure to support your courageous choices.

Revelations

- The act of revealing or dislosing as something not before realized

- God's disclosure of himself and his will to his creatures

- An instance of such communication as the Bible

- Blessed is one who reads aloud the words of his prophecy and blessed are those who hears and keep it written within it. For the time is near.

Revelation is an apocalyptic prophecy with an epistolary introduction which means revealing of diine mysteries so write down every vision you see and release the divine energy to oneself, God and the universe. Revelations is the ending or last book of the bible which is vivid imagery of disaster and suffering.

7 Major themes of the book of Revelations

1.   Crown of Life (Rev: 2:10)
The saints who remain faithful until the end will receive a "crown of life"
2.   War in heaven (Rev: 12:7)
The war in heaven is a spiritual war for our souls. Satan does not want the faithful to be saved
3.   Lamb of God (Rev 5:12) is the Alpha and Omega (Rev 21:6)
The Lamb of God is Jesus who slain, Jesus died for our sins. He has the power over time. The Alpha and Omega means the beginning and the end of times.
4.   The Harvest (Rev 14:15
Is the final day when all on earth will be judged for their works, wheather they are faithful or unfaithful
5.   A new heaven and new earth (Rev 21:1)
The earth and heaven we now know will be destroued. A new heaven and new earth will be a new home for the faithful.
6.   Tree of Life (Rev 22:2)
Jesus promised us eternal life. The leaves on the tree of life or for healing. Whoever eats of the tree can live forever, but they have to be in the heaven thats where the tree s. Only the faithful will be in heaven.
7.   Jesus is coming again (Rev 22:2)
The faithful are in the church of Christ, the church of the

bride of Christ. Jesus promised he would come again for his bride. The church will be clad when Jesus comes

bride of Christ. Jesus promised he would come again for his bride. The church will be clad when Jesus comes

10 Commandments

- Remain close to the great spirit

- Show great respect for your fellow beings

- Give assistance and kindness wherever needed

- Be truthful and hoenst at all times

- Do what you know to be right

- Look after the being of mind and body

- Dedicate a share of your efforts to the greater good

- Treat the Earth and all that dwell there with respect

- Work together for the benefit of all mankind

- Take full responsibility for your actions